ROYAL ARM
IN
LINCOLNSHIRE
CHURCHES

Georgian Arms in St. Mary's church,
Barton-upon-Humber

JENNIFER S ALEXANDER & GEOFFREY F BRYANT

PUBLISHED BY

WORKERS' EDUCATIONAL ASSOCIATION · BARTON ON HUMBER BRANCH

1990

Contents

List of plates

List of figures

A brief history of the Royal Arms in churches

Royal Arms were displayed at English churches before the Reformation (Jeavons 1963, p. 51) sometimes in stained glass, at other times as part of the sculptural decoration of the building, as for example at Westminster Abbey where a splendid series was including in the thirteenth century rebuilding (Hasler 1980, p. 151). Buildings commissioned by royalty would be expected to feature the Royal Arms, and again at the King's College Chapel in Cambridge, it forms the main sculptural ornament of the interior. Nearer home at Great Ponton the parish church tower, built in 1519 by a local merchant, has the Tudor Arms prominently displayed on the outside as a personal gesture of loyalty to the monarch.

The use of Royal Arms under consideration here is, however, the specific display of Arms to reflect the role of the monarch as head of the church, either in response to legislation or as a spontaneous action on the part of the parish.

It is logical to assume that Arms would be hung at and after the time when Henry VIII established himself as 'Supreme Head on Earth of the Church of England' but though an order to this effect seems likely none has been found and the only quoted Arms from his reign is not authenticated (see Hasler 1980, p. 87, footnote 1). So it is probably untrue, as many do, to suggest that their introduction into our churches was one of the results of that chain of largely political events which led to the break with Rome. Certainly churches were commissioning Royal Arms by the reign of Edward VI and churchwardens' accounts in Suffolk and Essex attest their purchase (Cautley 1934, p. 21-22). Unless these are to be seen as spontaneous displays of loyalty to a monarch (whose Act of 1547 depriving them of their chantry revenues can hardly have made him popular with the parishes), it would suggest that parish churches were at least encouraged to display the Royal Arms. They might have been seen as a way of adding some colour to the recently despoiled church interiors particularly at the chancel arch. In 1552 at Wandsworth in Surrey £4. 12s. 6d was 'Paid for pulling down the rood loft and setting up of the

Scriptures, that is to say, the Creation of the World, the Coming of Our Saviour Christ, the Beatitudes, the Ten Commandments, the twelve articles of our Belief, and the Lord's Prayer, the Judgement of the World, [and] the King's Majesty's Arms. (Cautley 1934, p. 22).

Certainly, the church in England now had a secular rather than ecclesiastical head but the first known official mention of Arms in churches seems to be in 1561 when Royal Orders suggested that an Arms would be 'a seemly cresting for the chancel arch'. They would thus suitably replace the 'Popish' Rood and Doom as the dominant visual image displayed to the eastward-facing congregation in the nave and reinforce those feelings of loyalty and affection which Englishmen increasingly felt for their monarch in and after the sixteenth century.

The accession of Henry's Catholic daughter Mary saw no definite orders to remove any Arms but, where necessary, they were 'to be removed from the altar and...set in a place more convenient' (Cautley 1934, p.24). Some were doubtless replaced by re-installed Roods, many others destroyed. Mary is the only monarch since the Reformation whose Arms do not appear officially in an English church.

However, as we have seen, in 1561, soon after her accession, Elizabeth (1558 - 1603) decreed that an Arms was a most suitable cresting for the again roodless chancel screen. Grantham's Elizabethan Arms of 1586, though now hanging on an aisle wall, is the earliest one preserved in a Lincolnshire church. The practice carried into the seventeenth century and George Abbott, Archbishop of Canterbury (1611 - 1633), issued licenses to approved painters who would 'survey and paynte in all the churches and chappells within the Realm of England Kings Majties Armes in due form, with helme, crest and Mantell and supporter's as they ought to be' (Blair and Evetts 1953, p. 50). No Arms of James I are preserved in Lincolnshire but Arms of Charles I (1625 - 49) are preserved at Boston, Haltham on Bain and Cotes by Stow (1635).

During the Commonwealth (1649 - 60) royalty was viewed with disfavour, Royal Arms were not displayed, and doubtless many existing ones were defaced or destroyed. A broadsheet dated April 9 1650 reads that it had been 'resolved by Parliament...that all Justices of the Peace etc...to cause the Arms of the late King to be taken down and defaced in all Churches' (Bretton 1955, p.93). At Uffington, Shropshire the Churchwardens paid 10s for 'ye Armes of ye comonwelth' (Pardoe 1987, p. 11) which Arms seem to have been a creation based on the flags of the separate parts of the United Kingdom (see Cautley 1934, fig. 27).

The restoration of Charles II soon produced a proclamation dated May 9 1660 which stated that 'the Arms of the Commonwealth, wherever they are standing be forthwith taken down; and that the King's Majesty's Arms be set up instead thereof' (Bretton, op.cit., p. 93). This order apparently only applied directly to the replacement of the Commonwealth Arms in Westminster with those of the new monarch (Hunter Blair and Evetts, 1953, p. 51) though some writers have suggested that it applied nation-wide and was more or less obligatory on all churchwardens. However, there is evidence that in many places Arms of Charles II were at this time newly placed in churches and Cautley cites nearly thirty examples

Plate 1. Arms of Charles II in Grantham parish church.

Plate 2. Detail of the James II Arms in Immingham church.

of this period still to be seen in Suffolk (Cautley 1934, p.46).
The 1661 Churchwardens' Accounts of St. John the Baptist Church,
Winchester record a payment of £1 4s 0d to one Giles Uphill for
the painting of the King's Arms and at the same time five pence to
'Lucas' for washing out the State's Arms (Pardoe 1987, p. 37), and
the parish registers of Warrington record in 1660 that 'it is
generally enjoined by the Great Counsell of England that in all
Churches thorowout the Kingdom of England his Majesties arms shall
be sett upp..' (Cautley 1934, p. 46).

So, after the Restoration of 1660, though not legally
compulsory, it became generally accepted that the Royal Arms
should be displayed in our churches and the second surviving Arms
at Grantham (Plate 1) are dated to the reign of Charles II (1660
- 85).

Charles' successor in 1685, James II, was soon seen to have
Catholic leanings and was fairly speedily removed in the Glorious
Revolution of 1688. In many ways Lincolnshire's most puzzling Arms
are those now hanging over the chancel arch at Immingham (Back
cover and Plate 2). Clearly dated 1688 and dedicated to 'J 2 R'

they are further inscribed 'FEAR GOD HONOUR YE KING'. Arms of this short, largely unpopular, reign are obviously rare (Cautley 1934, p. 53 - 4) and where dated the few surviving examples tend to be of 1685. So, did the population of Immingham have particularly Catholic leanings at this time, or was the church in the hands of a Catholic family or clique? Perhaps even the Arms may have been ordered from the painter early in James' reign but though delivered somewhat late they were still hung? And finally, could these 1688 Arms be unique?

Plate 3. Arms of William III in Fleet church.

No Arms of William and Mary (1689 - 94) survive in Lincolnshire but those at Fleet (Plate 3) dated 1698 are of William when he ruled alone (1694 - 1702) after the death of

Mary. Their virtual absence in Lincolnshire might be considered unusual for, unlike James, their accession did produce a change in the Royal heraldry and one or two more might be expected to have survived.

Arms of Queen Anne (1702 - 1714) survive, at Anwick (Plate 10), Cowbit (Plate 4), Harpswell, Humberston, Kirkby on Bain, Navenby, Owston Ferry and Surfleet (Plate 7), most of the period after the Union with Scotland in 1707. It is thought that the quite frequent occurence of this monarch's Arms may be associated with her popularity after 1704 when she founded the Queen Anne's Bounty.

The arrival of the Hanoverian monarchs, with their new heraldry including the quarter of Hanover on the shield, saw the authorities making strenuous efforts to ensure that the correct Arms were displayed in our churches, a move probably provoked by the strong Jacobite sympathies of many of the clergy and upper classes. If the obligation to display the correct Arms had been strenuously followed we would, of course, now have no early ones

Plate 4. Arms of Queen Anne in Cowbit church.

Plate 5. Arms of George II in Westborough church.

surviving. Thus vast bulk of Lincolnshire's (probably the country's) surviving Arms are of the Hanoverian monarchs - the first three Georges (Plates 5 and 6) and Victoria being well represented, George IV less common, and William IV only seen at Toynton All Saints and possibly Hemswell (Plate 26). Dating Hanoverian Arms of the first three Georges is often difficult, if not impossible, though increasingly churchwardens' names and signatures of painters, often with dates, do occur on the Arms during the eighteenth century and surviving churchwardens' accounts can be used.

Mention should here be made of the 'updating' of Arms which was certainly carried out during this period and would often save the churchwardens a considerable sum of money. An Arms hung for George the First and inscribed 'G R' could easily be given a '2' or 'II' on the accession of his son and the '3' inserted between the 'G' and the 'R' on the Arms at Thornton Curtis looks horribly suspicious. A most blatant piece of deception is that on the Arms at Horkstow where the date '1821' has been added to Arms which were clearly painted between 1714 and 1801. At Surfleet

(Plate 7), however, the deceit is even worse for here a
Royal Arms, clearly of Queen Anne from 1707 - 1714, has had the
initials G R IV added by a parish keen to economise and obviously
unconcerned with correct heraldry. Finally, mention might be made
of a similar, but more puzzling, case at St Martin's church,
Stamford where the Arms dates 1758 now clearly display the
heraldry of 1801 - 1816 (Plate 30). Surely, one would think, it
would have been easier, and less obvious, to change the date
rather than repaint the heraldry.

During the nineteenth century there seems to have been less need
to remind people of their loyalty to the Crown and the practice of
replacing out-of-date Arms apparently became less common.
However, it is interesting to note that in the late Georgian
churches built at such places as Carrington, Frithville and
Midville a display of Arms seems always to have been part of the
original furnishings. There, as elsewhere, they were generally
less elaborate Arms, often being of cast iron made from identical
moulds. Certainly this period saw a dramatic reduction in the

Plate 6. Arms of George III in Great Ponton church.

numbers of Arms hanging in our churches. They became unfashionable and large numbers were removed during the restoration work undertaken in most of our churches. Those

Plate 7. Arms of Anne (and George IV) in Surfleet church.

surviving were often moved to inconspicuous locations where they are now found, often having been totally neglected and badly in need of restoration.

Very. few sets seem to have been made for monarchs in the twentieth century and the practice seemed to have died out until the 1977 Jubilee celebrations for Elizabeth II when Moulton church, and several others in Britain, revived the tradition. The only other post-Victorian Arms in Lincolnshire seem to be those at Sutterton near Boston where an Arms of Elizabeth II dated 1981 has recently been hung though perhaps mention should also be made here of the replacement of the Arms lost in the Nettleham fire of 1969 (Plate 8).

Plate 8. Arms of 1816 - 1837 in Nettleham church,
repainted after the fire of 1969.

2.

Mechanism of Installation

How did the Arms get into our churches? The evidence available suggests that it was normally the churchwardens who organised the whole procedure and at Barton-on-Humber, Branston, Goxhill, Lincoln St. Benedict, North Somercotes and South Calton we have surviving documentary evidence, though only at Barton, South Carlton and Lincoln, St. Benedict have the Arms referred to survived [1].

[1] Gifts of Arms by individual doners are known, e.g. the Arms at Weston, Bath, Somerset are signed 'the gift of J. Jones, carver of this parish' (Pardoe 1987, p. 16).

Initially the wardens would have to approach a sign-painter [2]. He is likely to have been either itinerant or more likely a resident in a nearby town (Jeavons 1963, p. 54) as, for instance in Lincolnshire, Edward and Thomas Hunton of Lincoln, John Hawksworth and W. P. Pudsey of Gainsborough or C. Stout of Grimsby. These men were also employed to produce the many Commandment Boards, Lord's Prayers, Creeds, Moses and Aarons, hatchments and other mural paintings such as 'Sentences' which adorned Stuart and Georgian churches as evidenced below at Barton-on-Humber [3]. Bargaining apparently followed [4] as at North Somercotes (see below), Wirksworth and Chapel-en-le-Frith (Jeavons 1963, pp. 53-4). This would doubtless have determined the form and size of the Arms, the manner of production (perhaps paint on canvas or boards), the date of delivery, and the price to be paid. The wide range of prices which could be paid is seen in the extant documentary evidence set out below.

When the Arms were finished it might be necessary to pay someone to go to the painter's shop and bring them back to the church (see North Somercotes below), possibly incur further expense for a frame (see Goxhill and South Carlton below), and, finally, pay men such as blacksmiths and other helpers to hang the Arms in the church (see North Somercotes and Goxhill below).

The earliest extant documents referring to Arms are those dated 1672 in the long run of Churchwardens' Accounts for North Somercotes (LAO, North Somercotes Parish, 7) here reproduced. The right hand side of the document is damaged and fairly

[2] Obviously if the Arms required were to be in wood, plaster, stone or cast metal another craftsman or merchant would be contacted.

[3] See full details of the contract made with the painter Robert Summerfield of Wolverhampton by the Churchwardens of West Bromwich, Staffs which required him to produce King's Arms, Commandments, Lord's Prayer, Creed, Moses & Aaron and Sentences 'in Oyle Work only without Gold' by 'Christmas next' for the sum of £20 in Jeavons 1962, p. 88. The painters are also recorded variously as writers, gilders, picture cleaners, portrait, landscape, horse and cattle painters, inn sign painters, and carvers (Pardoe 1987) and they can sometimes be traced in local trade directories.

[4] The painter John Watson of King's Lynn was called to Northwold church in Norfolk in 1660 'to take the Kings Armes to paynt' but the Wardens recorded that 'wee could not agree with him' and they paid him two shillings 'towards his horse Journey'. Northwold's new Arms were painted in the same year by Samuell Masterman for £2 15s. 0d. (Pardoe 1987, p. 30).

certainly there was a column recording half-pennies spent - their
loss, if there were any, is hardly significant. The total
recorded cost was £1 .7s .6d.

They read:

The Account of Will Leach & Jo Kendall

Churchwardens of North Somercotes for the year 1672

	li	s	d
paid to the pantor for the Kings Arms drawing	1	3	6
spent with him when wee bargand with him	0	1	0
Given to a woman for bringing of the kings Arms home	0	1	0
paid to the blacksmith for Irons to hang them up by	0	1	0
spent of them that helpt to hang up the Kings Arms	0	1	0

   Also preserved (LAO Branston Par. 7) is a receipt dated March
30th 1724 for £6 4s paid to Abraham Hondius for the 'Kings
Armes the ten Comandments the Lords prayer and the Belefe' (Creed)
which he produced for Branston church.

In 1734 at St. Benedict's church Lincoln the Churchwardens' Accounts (LAO, Lincoln, St. Benedict Par.) record Jonathan Harrison and James Jelouss spending 18s and 2d for 'Bord for ye Armes', and £1 11s 6d 'for the King's Armes'.

No Arms are preserved in Goxhill church though they were still there when Archdeacon Bonney visited in 1846. However, the Churchwarden's accounts (LAO, Goxhill Par 7/1) show that in the year 1734-35 Arms were provided in the church.

	£	s	d
		3	0
	12	12	0
	2	2	0
	3	3	0
		2	6

'Drinke at John Marris takeing the Kings Armes	0	3	0
The Kings Court of Armes	12	12	0
The Frames	2	2	0
The Glory and the frames painting	3	3	0
Spent at John Marris Setting the Armes up	0	2	6'

The Goxhill wardens spent £34. 16 .0d during their year's office and it can be seen that the total spent on the Arms and their installation - £18 2s 6d - was over 50% of their total expenditure.

Although the actual Churchwardens' Accounts for the Barton-on-Humber churches have been lost entries from them were transcribed and have survived. [5] The earliest entries were probably of about 1650, the period when Royal Arms were, of course, out of favour. They read, 'bestowed on ale on the soldiers that came to deface the king's armes, 1s.' and 'to Martin Levitt, for washing out the king's armes, 1s.' Under the years 1660 - 61 is recorded, again perhaps not surprisingly, an account,

[5] Many entries were published by Canon W.E. Varah in numerous issues of the the Barton-on-Humber Parish Magazine. Copies of these are held in the Lincolnshire Archives Office. Other entries are in Ball, H. W., The Social History and Antiquities of Barton-on-Humber published in Barton in 1856.

'for the King's armes setting up' but the actual sum paid is not clear. However, another entry, 'spent of the painter when he painted the king's armes, 1s. 6d.' hardly hints at the production of a major work of art. Shortly afterwards a further charge of £1 15s. 3d. was recorded for further Arms painting perhaps to improve the originals. In 1740 the accounts of St. Peter's church noted that £26 was paid for painting a Royal Arms, the Lord's Prayer, Commandments, etc. and it seems clear that this must refer to the extant Arms preserved in Barton-on-Humber (Frontispiece) and for that price, not surprisingly, a quality piece.

At South Carlton in 1815 - 16 the churchwardens recorded the payment of £3 3s to Mr Patrick Shee 'for painting the Royal Arms for the Church' and a further 14s to Joseph Coxon 'for making, painting, and putting up the Frame for the Royal Arms'.

Finally, the Arms of 1981 hanging in the church at Sutterton were produced as a result of a gift by local resident Mr Albert Waite. In 1980 he left a legacy of £500 'which enabled the replacement of the Royal Arms and other benefits'. The details are recorded on a board in the church.

3.

The heraldry of the Royal Arms

The study of Royal Coats of Arms in churches cannot be undertaken without some knowledge of their heraldry. Heraldry has a terminology of its own which is here largely avoided. However, where it is used the word or words appear first in inverted commas though afterwards more familiar modern English equivalents are more frequently used. No pre-Tudor Royal Arms survive in Lincolnshire's churches but, for interest, we shall briefly consider the heraldry of the Arms from their starting point in the twelfth century.

The 'achievements of arms', the complete display, is made up of the elements outlined here - the escutcheon or shield, garter, helm, crown, mantling, crest, supporters, badges, and motto. Sometimes elements such as badges, crown and/or mantling may be omitted.

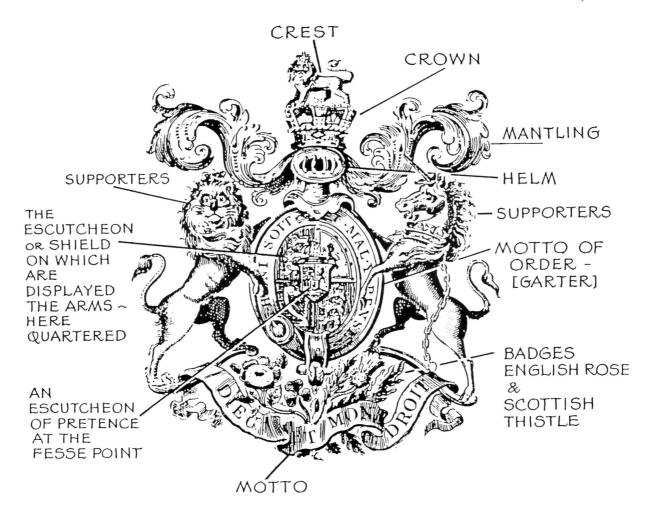

CREST

CROWN

MANTLING

SUPPORTERS

HELM

SUPPORTERS

THE ESCUTCHEON OR SHIELD ON WHICH ARE DISPLAYED THE ARMS ~ HERE QUARTERED

MOTTO OF ORDER - [GARTER]

AN ESCUTCHEON OF PRETENCE AT THE FESSE POINT

BADGES ENGLISH ROSE & SCOTTISH THISTLE

MOTTO

Fig. 1   The Royal Arms with its badges and emblems

The Arms of particular monarchs are recognised through study of the varying 'charges' on the 'escutcheon', that is, the designs or 'devices' within the quarters of the central shield. The quarters are numbered : 1 - top left; 2 - top right; 3 - bottom left; and 4 bottom right.

Knowledge of the changing designs will allow the reader to recognise and hopefully date any Royal Coat of Arms. The Royal Arms has always embodied the Arms of the territories that the monarchs have laid claim to and has hence changed over time. The medieval Royal Arms used by the kings of England from the late twelfth century is the simple one showing three 'lions passant guardant', that is, three lions walking on guard towards the left with the front right paw raised. They are really supposed to be leopards but are called lions in heraldry. They are painted 'or',that is gold, and shown on a 'gules', that is red, background. They still appear as part of the Royal Arms today. The Arms of France, golden fleurs-de-lys on a 'azure'/blue background first appeared on the English Arms under Edward III

Plate 9. Detail of the Arms in Somersby church showing
the French fleurs-de-lys in the second quarter.

after 1340, and remained part of the Arms until 1801 (Plate 9).
Until 1405 a large number of fleurs-de-lys was scattered over
the French 'device' but after that date only three appear.

The royal motto, 'Dieu et mon droit', God and my right, was
usually included in and after the reign of Henry VI (1422 - 1461)
but the Garter motto, 'Honi soit qui mal y pense', Shamed be he
who thinks evil of it, is earlier and dates from the reign of
Edward III (1327 - 1377).

Royal Heraldry in English churches

1. Early Arms to 1603 : here only Henry VIII (1509 - 1547); Edward VI (1547 - 1553); Mary (1553 - 1558); and Elizabeth (1558 - 1603)

In the first and fourth quarter are the 'devices' of France - in the second and third quarters those of England. Only the Arms at Grantham are of this period. Although the Arms remained the same during the period from c1406 to 1603 the supporters did change. During Henry VIII's reign they were generally to the 'dexter' (right side as seen looking from the rear of the Arms) a golden lion, and to the 'sinister' (left side as seen looking from the rear of the Arms) a red dragon of Wales.

2. Stuart Arms 1 of 1603 - 1688 and 1702 - 1707 : James I (1603 - 1625); Charles I (1625 - 1649); Charles II (1660 - 1685); James II (1685 - 1688); William and Mary (1688 - 1702, but see below); and Anne (1702 until the Act of Union of 1707)

After more than two and a half centuries during which the Royal Arms was virtually unaltered the 'devices' or designs on the central shield began to change fairly frequently after 1603.   Also, the Stuarts changed the right hand supporter from a Welsh dragon to a Scottish unicorn on James' accession. He was now king of England, Scotland, Ireland and 'France' so in the first and fourth 'grand quarters' (i.e. quartered quarters) appear the former shield with its English and French 'devices' as before. In the second, top right quarter, the shield of Scotland, a golden background on which appears a red 'rampant' lion inside a red decorated frame or 'tressure fleury counter-fleury'. This latter has two narrow parallel lines on which are fleurs-de-lys pointing inwards and outwards . In the third lower left quarter, Ireland, a golden harp with 'argent'/silver strings on a blue background. The motto on Arms of James I may read, 'Beati pacifi', Blessed are the peacemakers.

From 1654 to 1660 the Stuart Arms were abolished by the Commonwealth but they were brought back unchanged at the Restoration. The Commonwealth Arms, a form of 'State Arms', was based on the flags of the three parts of the United Kingdom (it omitted France) and had the personal Arms of Oliver Cromwell in the centre. It was 'blazoned' or decorated with, in the first and fourth quarters St George's cross, in the second quarter St Andrew's cross, and in the third quarter the Irish stringed harp. Cromwell's Arms were a silver rampant lion on a 'sable'/ black background.

During the reigns of William and Mary and then William alone the main shield may be further embellished by the addition 'in pretence' of William's own smaller arms of Nassau. On this there appears on a blue field a gold rampant lion and a number of small, upright, golden rectangles or 'billettees'. During the joint reign this appeared to the left of centre of the main shield but when he ruled alone it took a  position at the 'fesse point', that is, in the very centre where the four quarters meet and thus it became an 'escutcheon of pretence'.

3. Stuart Arms 2 of 1707 - 1714 : Queen Anne

After the Act of Union, 1707, the Queen's Stuart Arms were changed and England and France were for first time 'divorced'. Now England and Scotland appeared side by side - 'England impaling Scotland' - in the first and fourth quarters. France and Ireland filled the second and third quarters respectively. The motto now usually reads 'Semper Eadem', Always the same (Plate 10).

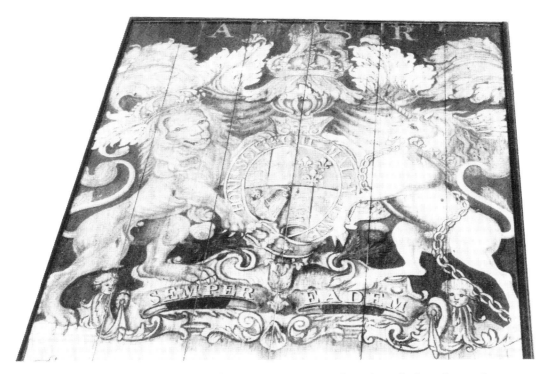

Plate 10. Arms of Queen Anne in Anwick church.

4. Hanoverian Arms 1 of 1714 - 1801 : George I (1714 - 1727); George II (1727 - 1760); and George III (1760 until 1801)

The first, second and third quarters are as before but the Arms of the new king, George Lewis, Elector of Hanover, now fill the fourth quarter (Plates 5 and 6). These latter arranged in a form known in heraldry as 'party per chevron and per pale' have, top left the Arms of Brunswick, two golden lions 'passant guardant' on a red background; top right for Luneburg, a blue lion 'rampant' surrounded by a number of red hearts - a 'seme of hearts gules' - on a gold background; and below, the Arms of Westphalia, a silver (perhaps white) horse galloping on a red background. In the middle of this shield a smaller shield, an 'escutcheon of pretence', containing the arms of office for the Arch-Treasurer of the Holy Roman Empire - a post which the Electors held - the golden Crown of Charlemagne on a red background.

5. Hanoverian Arms 2 of 1801 - 1816 : George III

In 1801 the Irish and English parliaments were united and a new Arms was decreed. George III decided to abandon his title of King of France so for the first time the fleurs-de-lys were removed from the English Arms (Plates 11, 12 and 24). England now appears in quarters one and four; Scotland in two; and Ireland in the third quarter. At the centre, or 'fesse point', there appears the Hanoverian Arms with the Electoral Bonnet 'ensigned' over. This was a red velvet cap with an ermine brim and a gold tassel on top.

Distinguishing between the Arms of the late Hanoverian kings is not easy as Bonnets and Crowns can be easily confused.

Plate 11. Arms of George III (1801 - 1816) in Harlaxton church.

6. Hanoverian Arms 3 of 1816 - 1837 : George III (1816 - 1820); George IV (1820 - 1830) and William IV (1830 - 1837)

Napoleon abolished the Holy Roman Empire and so went the states and the electoral princes. However, after the Congress of Vienna in 1814 Hanover became a Kingdom so from 1816 until 1837 a Royal crown replaced the Electoral Bonnet above the central Arms of Hanover (Plate 12).

Plate 12. Arms of 1816 - 1837 in Edenham church.

7. Arms of Victoria and all succeeding monarchs 1837 - present day

Women were unable to succeed to the Hanoverian throne (the Salic Law) so our Continental links were severed and the Victorian Arms are as before but with the central Hanoverian shield removed (Plates 13, 14 and 23). The Royal Arms have remained unchanged since this time.

Plate 13. Arms of Queen Victoria in Fleet church.

Plate 14. Arms of after 1837 in Market Rasen church :
cast metal type 1.

4.

Methods and materials

The materials used for the Royal Arms vary considerably but
canvas and wood are the most common. In some cases the Arms are
painted directly onto the plaster of the wall, usually above the
chancel arch. Cast metal first appears as a material in the early
eighteenth century, the Arms obviously mass-produced and not
intended solely for church use. Carved sets in high relief can be
found, made of wood, stone (including artificial Coade stone) and
even plaster. Examples of Royal Arms painted on sheet metal are
known in Lincolnshire (e.g. Wootton), but unlike the Commandment

tables sometimes found with Royal Arms sets, flat bed slate has
not been seen. The majority of Royal Arms sets in the region are
painted on canvas and then framed. Where wood is used the panel
is normally made up of a series of boards that are then framed.

Most Royal Arms are rectangular in shape, but a surprising
number are lozenge-shaped, like hatchments, and octagonal and
quatrefoil sets (see Leverton and Harlaxton, Plate 11) are also
known. To some extent the shape of the set was dictated by the
space it was going to occupy. In the eighteenth century they were
often meant to fill the space between the screen and the chancel
arch and were accompanied by boards or a large tympanum on which
were painted the Commandments, the Creed the Lord's Prayer, and
perhaps figures of Moses and Aaron. An enormous Arms
presumably shaped to fit below the church's chancel arch can be
seen at Aslackby.

Few Royal Arms now remain in their original setting in or above
the chancel arch and many are now to be found above the tower arch
or in various locations at the west end of the nave.
Unfortunately others are abandoned in dark corners, stacked with
the lumber and long forgotten. In common with the Commandments,
Creed and Lord's Prayer boards they have suffered greatly from
the re-orderings and restorations which have taken place in our
churches since the middle of the nineteenth century. Happily
there are indications that in recent years their artistic and
historical significance has become more appreciated and at
churches such as Immingham (see back cover), Grimsby and Horkstow
Arms have been carefully cleaned and/or restored.

5.

Painters and types of Royal Arms

Little is known about the identities of the painters of the
Royal Arms, but the signed examples do provide some clues. They
were frequently the work of local sign painters, listed in trade
directories under such headings as 'Painter, house and signs etc.'

Others worked in other trades as well. John Hawksworth of Gainsborough, who may have been responsible for updating the Royal Arms at Hemswell (Plate 26), is listed as a painter and coal merchant in Hager's 1849 Lincolnshire Directory, whilst Theophilus Simpson of Stamford is there described as a painter and victualler.

It is certain that these men were familiar with heraldry and it seems most likely that they were able to work from pattern books. They may also have painted hatchments, inn signs and livery badges on carriages and the like. In the case of Royal Arms it is probable that the College of Heralds issued drawings of the new heraldry at every necessary change. Another way in which the painters may have been provided with a sight of up-to-date Arms was by the churchwardens who would be in possession of Royal Proclamations issued to their churches for reading to the parishioners. These are heading with clearly printed contemporary Royal Arms. Certainly the painters were made aware of the changes with some speed, as is evident from still extant Arms at churches such as Billinghay (Plate 15) and Great Hale where correctly

Plate 15. Arms of George III in Billinghay church.

blazoned Arms are dated 1801 - the first year of a period when new heraldry was required.

Related sets of Royal Arms

1. Painted Royal Arms

(i) The 'Wave-form Mantling' group

There are several related groups of Royal Arms in the region, some obviously the work of one painter, others derived from a common source. The most interesting group, however, is the 'Wave-form Mantling' group that covers a considerable time range and is also known outside the region. The Royal Arms that constitute the group are all very nearly identical in style and handling, though of different heraldic periods. They embody the same characteristics in spatial arrangement of the elements of the Arms, the use of a particular type of motto frame, the form of the supporters, and of the mantling.

The group consists of Royal Arms from the reign of James II (1685 - 1689) to the reign of George III (1760 - 1820), with the majority displaying the Arms of the first Hanoverian period from 1714 to 1801. Analysis of the elements of each of the Royal Arms in the group reveals that although several sets may be the work of one painter, most are by separate artists.

The mantling is a very important part of the Arms of this group, occupying between a quarter and a third of the picture space. It is characterised by its three dimensional wave-like form, its arrangement within the Arms, and its colours - gold with an ermine lining. The mantling is fastened to the crown of the helm and sweeps out behind it in long loose folds with tattered scale-like edges. Behind the supporters it shows the ermine lining. It forms a tri-lobe that defines each of the top corners of the regular shape of the Arms. The first lobe sways violently upwards from a point half way up the helm to the level of the lion crest whilst the second section curls back upon itself above the supporters' heads to reveal the gold side and its tip then flicks up to show the ermine (Plates 10 and 15). The third lobe that shows the ermine occupies the space between each supporter and the edge of the picture space. The mantling occurs in precisely this form in every Royal Arms in the group with the exception of Barlings, where the painter has misunderstood the original he was copying and has produced mantling of tremendous energy but no coherent form. Wave-form mantling is only found in this group and the closest parallels to it are to be found in carved Royal Arms.

The supporters, although having detail differences, are virtually identical throughout the group. The lion and unicorn are shown as fierce, emaciated creatures, the latter especially so, with a strongly painted muscle structure. The lion is characterised by its long flowing mane and light feathering on its legs; the unicorn by its heavy neck, straggled mane and beard, and by its long elegant horn. Neither of the supporters is completely rampant, but both lean forward from a half crouched position to grasp the Garter motto surrounding the shield (Plates 21b and 22c).

The motto frame at the base of the Royal Arms of this group acts as a background to the motto ribbon as well as a stand for the supporters and is usually positioned above the plinth. These frames are perhaps the most varied parts of the Arms, allowing the painter some freedom of expression within specified bounds. The frame is present on all but one of the group, Horkstow, due perhaps to its lozenge shape.

The frame has the appearance of carved wood and is painted in a single colour perhaps to accentuate this. The top is dominated by two heavy scolls from which the rose and thistle badges emerge. The ends of the frame are finished in an acanthus scroll, topped by the head of a putto. The frame of the earliest example in the group, the 1688 Arms at Immingham (see back cover), terminates in strapwork characteristic of work of that date, whilst the Harpswell Arms of 1703 has scolls and putti on the most elaborate frame and base of the group. In each case a swathe of drapery hangs from the centre of the scroll. At Harpswell it loops down over the front of the tall plinth and meets one end of each of the two swags placed at either side of the monogram. In the majority of cases the lower edge of the frame is finished with further scrolls and scallop shells, much in the style of eighteenth century gilded frames.

The majority of Arms in the group date from the period 1714 to 1801 and a number of them are signed. These are : Navenby 1710 by Thomas Hunton of Lincoln; Firsby 1736 by Wm. Lambt. Clough; Barlings 1739 by Edw. Hunton of Lincoln; Orby in the Marsh 1781 by J.Burnitt; and Billinghay (Plate 15) 1801 by Everith. Additionally two sets are dated but not signed, Immingham, 1688 and Harpswell, and Harpswell, 1703. Royal Arms of this group are also known in other parts of the country. Abbey Dore in Herefordshire has a 1707 - 1714 set painted on the wall and Blankenham Parva in Suffolk has a James II set of 1685. Further examples doubtless await recognition.

It is remarkable that there should be sets of Royal Arms from a period as long as one hundred and twenty years, and by a number of different artists, that should be so similar. It is certain that the dates of the Royal Arms are correct in the majority of cases, and in some there is additional proof. At Abbey Dore for instance, the 1707 - 1714 set has actually been overpainted later in the eighteenth century by panels of texts, proving its date to be correct.

Stylistically there are detail changes that demonstrate that the Royal Arms in the group were painted when they seem to have been. The James II set at Immingham has the sort of strapwork on its motto frame that can also be found on contemporary woodcuts or on tomb monuments. Equally the later frames feature the type of design found on countless eighteenth century woodcarvings and depicted in paintings.

Pattern books and royal proclamations are the most obvious sources for royal heraldry, but the source for this group is perhaps more complex. The most striking feature of the group is their three-dimensional appearance, despite being painted on a flat surface. Lockington in Leicestershire (Plate 16) has a

Plate 16. Arms of Queen Anne in Lockington
church, Leicestershire.

magnificent Queen Anne Royal Arms above its chancel screen that embodies all the characteristics of the group, but is carved in high relief (apparently in plaster). The mantling makes more sense in high relief, with the centre of the three lobes breaking forward over the supporters' heads, and the plinth base of the whole set actually acts as the base of the whole Arms. Even the supporters are the same. It seems highly likely that the original design for the whole of this group was taken from a carved set and later used for painted examples.

(ii) W. P. Pudsey of Gainsborough

The churches of Kettlethorpe (Plate 27), Newton on Trent and Hemswell (Plate 26) each have a Royal Arms painted by William P. Pudsey. The first two are signed and the third can be shown to be (in part) by the same man. Newton's is the earliest set, signed 'Pudsey...Gainsboro 1792', and painted on a lozenge-shaped canvas. It shows Pudsey's elegant style to good effect, with effective use of its lozenge shape. The mantling, in red and silver, dominates the top of the Arms, rising high above the supporters' heads and falling in light, wave-like folds. The supporters are elegant slightly-built creatures, particularly the unicorn, with long arched necks, flowing manes and slender legs. The lion has a large head and a massive mane.

A particular device of Pudsey's is to show a faint shadow behind the chain 'reflexed', or hanging, over the unicorn's back; this can be seen on all three examples and is particular to Pudsey's work. The motto ribbon is divided into three sections and backed by an elaborate frame on the two square examples, with the frame depicted as a broken pediment beneath the Arms. The rose and thistle badges are shown at either side of the garter strap-end, painted as delicately as eighteenth century floral studies.

Kettlethorpe's set is also signed and dated - 'W. Pudsey pinxit Gainsboro 1812'. It is twenty years later than Newton's set but still embodies all the characteristics of Pudsey's style, this time in a square-shaped Royal Arms. The Hemswell set is an odd hybrid, clearly the work of two artists. The supporters, mantling and base very closely resemble the work of Pudsey, but the shield is the work of a second, less able artist. The heraldry is full of errors and the helmet above is out of line with the centre of the shield. The electoral bonnet has become a beehive and the helm itself is a diver's hard hat! There is a signature on the unicorn's flank, 'I. Hawkworth Painter Gainsbro 1837', in pencil that must be that of the second artist. The fact that the whole shield has been repainted suggests that the set must date from the 1714 - 1801 period originally, the same heraldry ar Newton's set. If it was changed from the second period, 1801 - 1816, to the third 1816 - 1837, then the changes needed would only have been slight.

William Pudsey is listed in the trade directories in Gainsborough from the 1790s to the 1820s at least, but the three sets of Royal Arms from west Lincolnshire are the only examples of his work known. It is possible that churches on the other side of the river Trent in Nottinghamshire may have other Royal Arms by Pudsey but one might expect to find more of his work in his native county. However, this part of the county has preserved very few Royal Arms and it appears to have been an area where churches were enthusiastically cleared in the nineteenth century restorations.

(iii) Complete list of known painters of Lincolnshire Arms

BRODDLE, Chris.	Arms of 1816 - 1837 at Nettleham repainted after the fire of 1969.
BULLARD	Arms of 1773 at Whaplode.
BURNITT, J.	Arms of 1781 at Orby in the Marsh.
CLOUGH, Wm. Lambt.	Arms of 1736 at Firsby.
COADE (of London)	Arms of 1820 at Edenham.
DESPIGHT, Terry	Arms of 1981 at Sutterton.
EVERITH	Arms of 1801 at Billinghay.
HAWKWORTH, I. (John) (of Gainsborough)	Repainted Arms at Hemswell in 1837.
HONDIUS, Abraham	Arms of 1724 at Branston - not extant.
HUNTON, Edw. (of Lincoln)	Arms of 1739 at Barlings.
HUNTON, Thomas (of Lincoln)	Arms of 1710 at Navenby.
SHEE or O'SHEE (of Newark)	Arms of c. 1815 - 1816 at South Carlton.
PHILLIPS, T. (of Bourne)	Arms of 1797 at Osbournby.
PUDSEY, W. P.	Arms of 1792 at Newton on Trent.
(of Gainsborough)	Arms of 1812 at Kettlethorpe.
	Probably Arms of 1801 - 1837 at Hemswell.
STOUT, C. (of Grimsby)	Arms of 1819 at Brigsley.
TROTTER, Cha.	Arms of 1733 at Aubourn.

2. Cast Metal sets

Cast metal Royal Arms first appear in the eighteenth century. Techniques of mass-production and a growing demand for Royal Arms from secular as well as church authorities resulted in large numbers of sets being produced. Sales seem to have been fairly widespread, with examples from the same mould appearing in Sussex and Herefordshire as well as Lincolnshire.

The Lincolnshire cast metal sets are from three different moulds, with further examples of all three of them recorded in other counties.

Type 1.

This is a fairly small Arms, measuring 18 inches by 16 inches and is in half-relief. The mantling is simplified and consists of two upward-curving swathes that rise from the base of the helm and double back on top of the supporters' heads. Examples from this mould are found from the first Hanoverian period (1714 - 1801) at Swaston in Cambridgeshire and at Hitchen in Hertfordshire (pers. comm. from Rosemary Pardoe) but none of this early date have been recognised in Lincolnshire.

The known Lincolnshire examples mostly date from the 1801 - 1837 period, (Plate 17) with three from post 1837. It is really quite difficult to date the Lincolnshire sets more closely owing to the representation of the 'crown' above the Hanoverian shield. In each example the 'crown' is shown as an amalgamation of the electoral bonnet used from 1801 - 1816, and the crown proper used afterwards. Most of these sets have been painted in heraldic colours and the artist has usually chosen which way to depict the 'crown'.

Plate 17. Arms of 1801 - 1816 in Cherry Willingham church - cast metal type 1

Type 1 cast metal Arms are preserved in the late Georgian churches at at Carrington (1816), Midville (1819) and Frithville (1821) and are likely to have been part of their original furnishings.

Of the post 1837 sets from this mould, one at Snelland is on a shaped board with the initials 'V R' and the other two are not identified to the reign. It is apparent that this type of Royal Arms has met with continued royal approval since a post 1837 set is currently in place on the Royal Yacht Britannia.

Type 2

The second type of cast metal Royal Arms is considerably larger than type 1 and measures about 5 feet by 4 feet. It is hollow backed in half relief. The mantling consists of fronds of foliage, often painted green, rising from the top of the shield. All the sets seen are from the post 1837 period. There are four examples in churches in the region at Fishtoft, Saxby All Saints (Plate 18), Hougham by Louth and Nettleton, and one seen in secular use on a pub, the 'Lion and Royal' at Navenby. Peterborough Museum has two examples from this mould, of unknown origin (ibid.), and several can be seen above shops in King's Lynn which have the Royal appointment.

Plate 18. Arms of after 1837 in Saxby All Saints church - cast metal type 2.

Type 3

These are similar in size to type 1 but have a more three-dimensional treatment of the Arms. The base of the set is very elaborate, with the motto ribbon supported by stylised foliage. The shield has an elegantly scrolled edge. Only one example from this mould can be seen in the county, at Scawby,

(Plate 19) but a further six sets have been seen elsewhere, some in secular use (ibid.)

Plate 19. Arms of after 1837 in Scawby church
- cast metal type 3.

There are surprisingly few other sets of related Royal Arms in the county. The sets at Leasingham and Coleby (both unsigned) look very much like the work of one painter and both date from 1801 - 1816. They may be by the same artist as the sets at Farthingstone and Tiffield in Northamptonshire. Similarly, the Arms at Irnham and Corby Glen seem likely to be the work of one painter. Four Royal Arms in churches near Grantham are clearly related. Long Bennington (Plate 28), Foston, Stragglethorpe and Westborough (Plate 5) each have a Royal Arms, respectively painted with 1737, 1767, G R and 1757. Westborough's set is the finest, with the other three much cruder, and would have looked like the source for them but for its date. Instead it seems they all shared a common source and the Westborough painter was a more competent artist. Certainly they all share the same error, with three lions cramped into the Brunswick quarter instead of the more correct two and are further noteworthy (see Plate 21c) because the lion has his tongue sticking out!

The survival of Royal Arms in the churches is of course random. About one in six of the county's churches has a set, but distribution over the area is very patchy with some areas producing only a few. Royal Arms were never meant to be permanent, but should have been replaced at the accession of a new monarch.   In several cases this has resulted in two Royal Arms surviving in one   church   as at Grantham, Fleet and Boston.   South Carlton church is probably more representative of the usual practice.   Here   the   churchwardens' accounts for 1816 made reference to the removal of the old Arms, in this case for Queen Anne, to make room for a new set.

In many cases the Royal Arms must have been left until they collapsed from old age, dirt and decay, and then either replaced or just destroyed.   The fate of the Royal Arms left in dark corners and amongst the lumber is unlikely to be different unless an interest is taken in them.   It would be a shame if these interesting and colourful paintings were to disappear from the churches they have adorned for over four hundred years.

6.

Lincolnshire Royal Arms - a summary

There are over a hundred Royal Arms to be found in the churches of the diocese of Lincoln, covering the period from Elizabeth I to Elizabeth II. The majority of the sets are from the Hanoverian first period from 1714 to 1801, but other periods are well represented and there are a number of Stuart sets including a very rare one for James II.

The only Tudor Royal Arms in the county is in the parish church of St. Wulfram at Grantham and is for Elizabeth I. The Arms and supporters are those of several Tudor monarchs, but the date '1586' with 'E R' and the substitution of 'Vivat Regina' for the motto identify this set for Elizabeth. Swags of fruit and foliage such as one finds on sixteenth century sculptured panels are attached to the edges of the motto frame of the Arms and also to the Arms of the town in the base.

There are fourteen Stuart Royal Arms with all the monarchs of that House represented except James I. All these Royal Arms have been treated very decoratively and have elaborate motto frames but are clearly the work of different artists. The Boston set has the rose and thistle badges used as sources of extensive foliage that covers the whole lozenge behind the supporters.

Four of the Stuart sets are Charles I or II, with Cotes the only set indisputably for Charles I, the others being initialled 'C R'. Grantham's Stuart set (Plate 1) is inscribed 'C 2 R' for Charles II, unless the '2' is additional. Boston's set has 'C R' at its top, with both initials crowned and the motto 'Feare God, honour the King' in the base. Considering the Parliamentary sympathies of Boston during the Civil War it is unlikely that this set is for Charles I and it more probably dates from after 1660.

Immingham church has a rare Royal Arms (back cover and Plate 2) from the reign of James II, although it can only be identified to James by the initials and a date of 1688 above the Stuart heraldry. Fleet's set (Plate 3) dated 1698 is from the time of William and Mary, but after the death of Mary since it shows the heraldry used after 1694. The treatment of the whole subject is handled very decoratively and the lion supporter seems to have a human portrait head.

Queen Anne, the last of the Stuarts, assured her reputation in the eyes of the church and its parishioners by restoring to their use the first-fruits and tenths which had been 'nationalised' by Henry VIII. Doubtless this generosity accounts for the fairly widespread provision of her Arms in our churches and eight remain in Lincolnshire, a few survivors of what must have been a larger number. For example in South Carlton church there is now a Georgian Royal Arms, but there are extant records of the purchase of a Queen Anne set (LAO, South Carlton Parish 13). Two of the Lincolnshire sets, at Harpswell and Humberston, are from the early period of the reign before 1707 when the Stuart Arms was used, and the rest from 1707 - 1714. The two earlier sets are linked by their extensive use of gilding and very rich treatment, although they are not by the same artist. Surfleet's set (Plate 7), of the later period, is perhaps the finest of all the Queen Anne sets, with its use of elegant scroll-like mantling that resembles embroidery work, and a highly decorated motto frame.

From 1714 to 1837 the Royal Arms included the Arms of Hanover and only changed four times during the period. There are at least seventy seven sets of Royal Arms in the county from this period, the majority falling in the first part from 1714 to 1801.

The shapes that the panels of the Royal Arms assumed in the eighteenth century are remarkably varied, with sets shaped to fit into arches, and even unusual shapes like quatrefoils becoming

common.   Often tables of Commandments accompany the Royal Arms
and, as in the case of Rowston, take on a major importance in the
role of furnishings in the church.   Landscape backgrounds also
appear, as at Scothern, Harlaxton (Plate 11) and several other
places where they replace the mantling behind the Arms.

Carved wooden Royal Arms are more common during the eighteenth
century, frequently high-relief carvings of great skill and
considerable size.   The massive set at Great Hale was once part of
an immense group of Arms and Commandments that must have dominated
the interior of the parish church.   Cast metals Arms also make
their first appearance in the eighteenth century.

The period after 1837, the accession of Queen Victoria, is
perhaps the least interesting for the study of Royal Arms in the
county.   Standards of painting declined (although crudely painted
sets can be found in all periods), and more mass-produced cast
metal sets were acquired. The Royal Arms in Gainsborough parish
church (Plate 24) is painted to resemble a carved set with the
Arms casting a shadow on its background.   The Arms also obey
hatchments rules, with the shield presented as a lozenge and the
crest omitted, as if for an armigerous lady (but one who has
died).

Plate 20. Arms of Queen Victoria in St. John
the Evangelist church, Manthorpe, Grantham.

A simplified form of the Royal Arms seems to have been used after 1837 in a number of churches in the county. Manthorpe church near Grantham (Plate 20) has a Royal Arms that misses out the supporters and mantling in a set dated 1848, and Wooton has a set that is even further simplified. It has merely a shield with a crown above it and the motto 'Fear God honour Ye Kyng' and seems to be painted on sheet metal. There are twenty one post-1837 Royal Arms in the diocese of Lincoln, of which nine are of cast metal.

7.

Surviving Royal Arms in Lincolnshire churches

The date of the Arms or the monarch where shown on the Arms is indicated.

Pre 1603

Grantham (ER 1586)

1603 - 1688

Boston (C R); Cotes by Stow (1635); Grantham (C 2 R);Haltham on Bain (C R) and Immingham (1688)

1688 - 1702

Fleet (W R 1698).

1702 - 1707

Harpswell (1703); Humberston

1707 - 1714

Anwick (1708); Cowbit (1713); Kirkby on Bain (1712); Navenby (1710); Owston Ferry and Surfleet (A R - and also G R IV)

1714 - 1801

Addlethorpe (G R); Aslackby; Aubourn (1733); Barlings (1739); Barton upon Humber (G II R); Baumber; Braceborough; Burgh le Marsh (G R); Burton upon Stather (G 3 R); Corby Glen (G R); Cranwell (G 2 R); Crowland (1775); Firsby (1736); Foston (1767); Fulstow (1768); Grainsby (G R or G III R); Great Grimsby (G R); Great Ponton (G III R); Haceby; Harmston (1717); Holbeach (G II R); Horbling; Horkstow (G R but also dated 1821); Irnham (1726); Kirkby cum Osgodby (G 2d R); Kirkby Underwood; Leverton (W IV R and date 1823 added); Lincoln, St. Benedict (1734); Long Bennington (1737); Melton Ross (1774); Newton on Trent (1792); North Thoresby (1722); Norton Disney (G III R); Orby in the Marsh (1781); Osbournby (1797); Rowston (G R II); Scothern (1796); Somersby; Stragglethorpe (G R); Thornton Curtis (1768); Thorpe St. Peter (G R); Washingborough (G R); Well (G II R); Westborough (1757); Whaplode (1773) and Wyberton (G R).

1801 - 1816

Barnoldby le Beck; Billinghay (1801); Cherry Willingham; Coleby (G R); Deeping St. James; Great Hale (1801); Great Sturton (1808); Harlaxton; Kettlethorpe (1812); Leasingham; South Carlton (1816); Stamford, St. Martin (1808 - but painted over 1758); and Toynton All Saints (but dated 1831).

1801 - 1837

Stixwould

1816 - 1837

Belton by Grantham; Boston; Branston; Brigsley (1819); Carrington; Edenham (1820); Frithville; Hemswell(1837); Ingoldmells; Midville; Nettleham (but renewed post 1969); South Kelsey (G R IV); Tealby (G III R); Thurlby by Bourne; Wainfleet St. Mary; and Welton by Lincoln (with 1838 in base).

Post 1837

Canwick; East Stockwith; Fishtoft; Fleet (1867); Gainsborough; Grantham, St John Evangelist (1848) Hackthorn; Haugham; Market Rasen; Moulton (?1977); Nettleton; Raithby; Saxby All Saints; Scawby; Snelland (V R); Sutterton (1981); Sutton Bridge; Trusthorpe (1842), and Wootton.

Arms of unknown date

Rippingale

Plate 21. Lion supporters on Arms at a. Thorton Curtis,
b. Immingham, c. Foston and d. Washingborough.

Plate 22. Unicorn supporters on Arms at a. Baumber,
b. Braceborough, c. Leverton and d. Barnoldby le Beck.

8.

An Inventory of the surviving Royal Arms in Lincolnshire Churches

taken by Jennifer Alexander, Ro and Geoff Bryant, Elsie and Ron Newton,and Eleanor and Rex Russell [6].

Key

K = Kesteven; Ho = Holland; L = Lindsey; Hu = Humberside.

1. ADDLETHORPE, St. Nicholas (L) :
Over the north door of the nave. Painted on boards in a heavy 18th century frame; badly faded - needs restoring. Approx 70" square. Arms of 1714 - 1801, wave-form mantling sub-group, with banner supported by cherubs inscribed 'G R' and above:

> Let every soul be subject
> unto the higher Powers
> ROM XIII.i.

Before the 1936 restoration the Arms were hanging on the east wall of the nave with Commandments on either side - here the chancel was demolished in 1706, cf. Ingoldmells. Terrier of 1822 includes, 'The King's Arms with the 10 Commandments'(LAO Addlethorpe Parish 1).

2. ANWICK, St. Edith (K) :
Under tower, wood c. 4' by 7' trimmed on left and right edges with part of lion supporter's tail missing and return curves of mantling reduced (Plate 10). Arms of 1707 - 1714, in good condition, 'A R' above Arms and 'God Save the Queen of Great Britain 1708'. Wave-form mantling subgroup.

3. ASLACKBY, St. James (K) :
North-west of nave, canvas c.10' by 12' and shaped to fit an irregular archway -likely to have been the chancel arch. Arms of 1714 - 1801 in poor condition. A background of curtains pulled back. An architectural base beneath the motto ribbon, with putti motto supporters apparently having portrait heads. Wave-form mantling subgroup.

4. AUBOURN, Old Church (K) :
On chancel east wall. Canvas c.4' by c.3' in good condition though needs cleaning. Arms of 1714 - 1801 with 'G R' above Arms and 'Dennis Clarke (?) Will. Lambe Sidesman Cha. Trotter of Lincoln Painter 1733' beneath. Wave-form mantling subgroup.

5. BARLINGS, St. Edward (L) :
On the south wall of the nave. Painted on canvas backed with wood - faded, somewhat damaged and has woodworm. Rectangular 81" wide and 64" high including frame. Arms of 1714 - 1801 with 'G R 2d' across the top; '17 39' across the middle; and mid- bottom 'Edw Hunton of Lincoln Painter'. Wave-form mantling subgroup.

6. BARNOLDBY LE BECK, St. Helen (Hu) :
West end of nave above the tower arch. Painted on boards which unusually lay horizontally - about 2' square and in fairly good condition. Arms of 1801 - 1816. Mantling depicted as fronds of green foliage at the top of the shield and supporters shown crawling from behind it (Plate 22d). There is no crest and there are several errors in the heraldry, Scotland's lion is shown gold on a blue ground, the Luneburgh lion has changed colours with its ground, the Brunswick lions have a blue ground instead of a red one and the crown of Charlemagne is also against a blue ground instead of a red one.

7. BARTON-UPON-HUMBER,St. Peter's (Hu) :
The now lost Churchwardens' Accounts for Barton-on-Humber (see Ball, H. W., 'The Social History and Antiquities of Barton-on-Humber', Barton 1856, Part 2, pp.6 - 9) record the painting of Arms in 1660 and 1740. It is not possible to show for which church the 1660 Arms were painted but as Ball only saw Accounts dated 1740 for St. Peter's church the later Arms must have hung in that church and is doubtless the extant Arms of 'G II R' still preserved in the town (Frontispiece). It is not known when the Arms left St. Peter's but the parish magazine of 1890 (part ix) recorded its presence over the chancel arch in St. Mary's church. From then on the Arms

[6] This inventory does not include examples of Royal Coats of Arms produced in stained glass. Such Arms, of post 1837, do exist in windows at Lincoln St. Benedict, North Thoresby and High Toynton churches but the exact number is unknown to the authors.

had a chequered history within that church before being illegally sold in 1980; being restored at Gateshead Technical College in 1981-82; and subsequently becoming the subject of a Constistory Court in 1985. The Arms now (1990) hang in Baysgarth Museum in the town but permission has been gained for its re-hanging in St. Peter's church. Painted on canvas, c. 6' by 5'unframed. Arms of 1714 - 1801 with 'G II R' across the top. In very good condition, Wave-form mantling subgroup.

8. BAUMBER, St. Swithin (L) :
On east wall of nave above the chancel arch. Painted on canvas, c.5' by c.3', in good condition. Arms of 1714 -1801.

9. BELTON BY GRANTHAM,
    SS Peter and Paul (K) :
On porch north wall above the entrance to the church. Carved stone c. 2' 6" square and unpainted. Arms of 1816 - 1837 in good condition with 'Fear God, Honour the King' on the lower edge.

10. BILLINGHAY, St. Michael (K) :
On the west wall of the nave. Painted on canvas. Arms of 1801 - 1816 (Plate 15). Forms the base of a large set of Commandments torn away from the frame at the lower edge. The Arms are against a blue background with curtains pulled back to reveal it. 'G III R' above the Arms; 'Anthony Radford Churchwarden 1801 Everith Painter' in base. Wave-form mantling subgroup.

11. BOSTON, St. Botolph (Ho) :
On south west wall of nave. Stuart Arms on wood c. 6' side on a lozenge. Needs cleaning. 'C R' above the Arms with crowns on both initials, 'Feare God Honour the King' beneath. Mantling ermine and or.
12. On nave north wall an Arms of 1816 - 1837 in cast iron, painted. Type 1 complete.

13. BRACEBOROUGH, St. Margaret (K) :
On porch north wall above the entrance to the church. Painted on wood, c. 4' by c. 3', Arms of 1714 - 1801. An error in the heraldry, the tressure of Scotland blue instead of red. In good condition, mantling ermine and or and swags of foliage under the motto ribbon.

14. BRANSTON, All Saints (K) :
On the organ case. Cast metal, painted, type 1 complete Arms of 1816 - 1837. Errors in the quarter of Hanover; the Luneburgh lion is red instead of blue and the horse of Westphalia is against a blue ground instead of a red one. Mantling painted ermine and or. Branston has previously had a Georgian Arms, together with Commandments, Creed and Lord's Prayer, for which Abraham Hondius, the painter had been paid £6 . 4s 0d in 1724 (LAO Branston Parish 7).

15. BRIGSLEY, St. Helen (Hu) :
On the north wall of the nave. Painting on boards - rectangular 4' 6" wide, 3' 9" high. Good condition. Arms of 1801 - 1837 - lacking bonnet in the middle of, and the crown on top of, the Hanover Arms. In bottom left corner, 'C. Stout, Grimsby, 1819', so should be George III. Loft saw it soon after it was installed (LAO, Dixon 19/1/2, p.66) and noted that it was 'over archway' and 'very indifferently executed'. The supporters are emerging from behind the achievement, the lion crouching low and the unicorn proudly upstanding. Above the garter a large crown and the three great feathers of the Prince of Wales. Inside the garter the achievement slopes backwards to the left. A note below reads 'Coat of Arms of George IV when he was the Prince of Wales but he kept it when he became King and there was no Prince of Wales to succeed him for some years'. Pardoe:'the painting itself is especially interesting as it seems to be an attempt by the artist to paint the Arms of the Regency.' She indicates that in her experience it is unique.

16. BURGH LE MARSH, SS Peter & Paul(L):
On tower north wall. Painted on wood c. 5' 6" by c.4'. There are several long vertical cracks in the wood and the paint has become bitumanised in some areas. Arms of 1714 - 1801 with 'G R' above. Error in Hanover quarter where crown of Charlemagne and its ground have exchanged colours. Mantling ermine and or. Wave-form mantling subgroup.

17. BURTON-ON-STATHER, St. Andrew (Hu) :
Above the nave north door. Painting on canvas about 3' square. Fairly good condition. Arms of 1714 - 1801, across the top 'G 3 R'.

18. CANWICK, All Saints (K) :
Above the chancel arch. Plaster (?), about 2' square (Plate 23). Arms of post 1837. Painted but with the tressure of Scotland painted blue instead of red. No crest or mantling but in good condition.

Plate 23. Arms in Canwick church.

19. CARRINGTON, St. Paul (L) :
On the front of the western gallery.
Cast metal, painted black, Type 1, cf.
Frithville, though here not in such
good condition with lion supporter's
right foot and part of associated ribbon
broken off and mantling above unicorn's
head damaged. Arms of 1816 - 1837 so no
doubt placed in the church when it was
built in 1816.

20. CHERRY WILLINGHAM, SS Peter and Paul
(L) :
Over the west door. Cast metal and
painted in colours, in fair condition
(Plate 17). Arms of 1801 - 1816, type 1
complete.

21. COLEBY, All Saints (K) :
On nave west wall. Painted on canvas c.
4' by c.3'. Arms of 1801 - 1816 in good
condition but needs cleaning. 'G R'
above Arms. Mantling ermine and or.

22. CORBY GLEN, St. John Evangelist (K) :
On nave west wall. Lozenge-shaped, c.3'
side - high up and dark. Arms of 1714 -
1801 with 'G R' in upper angle. Similar
Arms at Irnham.

23. COTES-BY-STOW, St. Edith (L) :
On the north wall of the nave opposite
the doorway. Painted on boards c. 4'
wide and 4' 6" high. Very worn. Arms of
Charles I dated '1635' across the top.

24. COWBIT, St. Mary (Ho) :
Above nave north door. Painted on
canvas c.3' 6" by c.3' in good condition
(Plate 4). Arms of 1707 -1714 with 'A R'
above Arms and '1713' beneath. Motto
'Semper Eadem'. Mantling ermine and or.

25. CRANWELL, St. Andrew (K) :
On nave south wall. Painted on wood 2'
by 1' 9". Arms of 1714 - 1801 with 'G 2
R' above; in good condition though
heavily varnished. Wave-form mantling
subgroup. Restored in 1973.

26. CROWLAND, Abbey church (Ho) :
On nave south wall. Painted on canvas
c.4' square. Arms of 1714 - 1801 in
sound condition though needs restretch-
ing. '1775' above Arms. Errors in
Hanover, shield with crown of
Charlemagne missing and lower lion of
Brunswick given extra back legs.
Luneburgh lion red instead of blue.

27. DEEPING ST JAMES, St. James (K) :
On nave west wall. Cast metal, painted
Arms of 1801 - 1816, type 1 complete.
Mantling ermine and or.

28. EDENHAM, St. Michael (K) :
Above the chancel arch. Carved in
artificial stone on rectangular block
c.6' by 4' and painted (Plate 12). Arms
of 1816 - 37 with very small amount of
mantling. Signed 'Coade : London :
1820'. Errors in colouring, Scotland has

a blue ground with gold lion and
tressure, and Luneburgh's lion and semee
of hearts are both gold.

29. EAST STOCKWITH, St. Peter (L) :
Over west door of nave (church is
orientated north-south). Carved in wood
and mounted on board c.28" square. Arms
of post 1837 in good condition.

30. FIRSBY, St. Andrew (L) :
Not in church at present. Arms of 1714
- 1801 painted on canvas c.4' 8"
square. 'Mr Wm Hetherington Churchwarden
1736' in base with 'Wm Lambt Clough
Pinxy' at lower right. Wave-form
mantling subgroup. At present at College
of Art, Lincoln.

31. FISHTOFT, St. Guthlac (Ho) :
On nave west wall. Cast metal Arms of
post 1837. Type II complete and
painted.

32. FLEET, St. Mary Magdalen (Ho) :
Over south door of nave. Painted on
canvas c.5' side, lozenge-shaped (Plate
3). Arms of William III after the death
of Mary - in sound condition. 'W R'
above Arms, 'W Jay J Fisher 1698'
beneath in cartouche supported by
cherubs. Lion supporter appears to have
human face, possibly a caricature. Helm
above shield decorative non heraldic
type. Mantling ermine and or.
Illustrated in Munro Cautley (1934), pl.
40.
33. On tower east wall. Arms painted on
sheet metal, c.2' 6" by c.2'. Arms of
post 1837 with 'V R' above and '1867'
below (Plate 13). Errors in heraldry.
Lions passant in first and fourth
quarters face the wrong way and
Scotland's tressure has been replaced by
a field of hearts. No mantling or
crest. There is a hole in the centre of
the Arms - somewhat crude.

34. FOSTON, St. Peter (K) :
Above chancel arch. Painted on canvas
c.3' 6" by 3' and in good condition.
Arms of 1714 - 1801 with 'G III R' above
and '1767' below). Mantling ermine and
or. Error in Hanover quarter where
Brunswick has three lions instead of
two. Rather crude set perhaps related
to the 1757 set at Westborough and the
Long Bennington and Stragglethorpe sets.

35. FRITHVILLE, St. Peter (L) :
High on the west wall of the nave. Cast
metal, painted black, 20" wide and 18"
high, cf. Carrington type 1, but in very
good condition. Arms of 1816 - 1837 and
so probably placed in the church when it
was built in 1821.

36. FULSTOW, St. Lawrence (L) :
On the north wall of the nave. Painting
on canvas over boards - 4' 4" square .
Fairly well preserved. Arms of 1714 -
1801 across the top of which 'G III R
1768' and below, 'Wm Ludham
Churchward' (sic).

37. GAINSBOROUGH, All Saints (L) :
On west gallery. Painted on canvas 2' 3" square. In good condition (Plate 24). Arms of post 1837 on lozenge without crest or mantling.
Hanging in the Great Hall at Gainsborough Old Hall is a large Arms of 1801 - 1816. Painted on canvas, 70" high and 64" wide. In good condition. Did this hang in the church prior to the hanging of the Arms above?

Plate 24. Arms in Gainsborough church.

38. GRAINSBY, St. Nicholas (L) :
Behind the door on the south wall of the nave. Painting on boards - lozenge-shaped, 3' square. Very indistinct as it badly needs cleaning. Arms of 1714 - 1801 with 'G R' to left and right. Loft recorded (LAO Dixon 19/1/2, p. 64) that in 1826 there was an Arms of G. R. III dated 1804 over the screen. If the extant Arms are the ones which Loft saw neither the 'III' or the '1804' are visible today and in any case would appear to have been additions to an Arms most probably of George I [see also Horkstow below].

39. GRANTHAM, St. Wulfram (K) :
On nave south wall at east end. Painted on wood, c. 3' 6" side on a lozenge. Tudor Arms with lion and dragon supporters. Good condition with 'E R' above Arms and '1586' to left and right, 'Vivat Regina' in place of motto. Arms beneath chequy sable and or within bordure erminois, for Grantham. Set without crest or mantling.
40. On nave south wall at west end. Painted on wood c. 3' 6" side on a lozenge (Plate 1). Stuart Arms in good condition. 'C R' to left and right of Arms with '2' above the crest. Shield rounded to fit within Garter ribbon. Mantling ermine and or. Arms of Grantham beneath.

41. GRANTHAM, Manthorpe, St. John Evangelist (K) :
On nave north wall. Wood, c. 3' across with semicircular projections. Arms of post 1837 in good condition with 'V R' to left and right of the Arms and '1848' below (Plate 20). Arms without crest, mantling, supporters or motto ribbon are set within garter ribbon with crown above. Red rose, thistle, white rose and shamrock badges. Church guide says Arms were a gift of Henry Francis Cust.

42. GREAT GRIMSBY, St. James (Hu) :
Above the door of the south aisle. Painting on canvas - c. 6' square. Arms of 1714 - 1801 with 'G R' beside Arms in elaborate lettering. In good condition - restored in 1981/82 by Ben Lyte of Caythorpe, near Grantham who states that the Arms were previously restored, c. 1850. Somewhat unheraldic treatment with the supporters crawling from behind the Arms, and the Prince of Wales' feathers above the crown instead of the Royal crest and mantling. Errors in the Hanover quarter with Luneburgh lion red instead of blue and the crown of Charlemagne red on silver instead of gold on red.

43. GREAT HALE, St. John Baptist (K) :
Over nave north door. Carved and painted on wood c.7' 6" wide. Arms of 1801 - 1816 with lower edge defined by edge of motto ribbon and '18 GIII 01' above Arms. In good condition and a very fine set. Photo in church of the west end before restoration shows the Arms positioned above the west gallery.

44. GREAT PONTON, Holy Cross (K) :
In nave, on south-west wall. Painted on canvas c.4' side. Arms of 1714 - 1801 (Plate 6). In good condition with 'G III R' above the Arms. Mantling ermine and or.

45. GREAT STURTON, All Saints (L) :
On south wall of nave. Painting on boards - 59" wide, 49" high in Venetian window form. Very good condition - restored post 1977. Arms of 1801 - 1816 with 'G R' in pediment and across the bottom 'JOSEPH RICHARDSON 1808 CHURCHWARDEN'. Richardson was Church-warden from 1772 - 1808.

46. HACEBY, St. Margaret (K) :
Above the chancel arch. Painted on the wall plaster c.6' by c.4'. Arms of 1714 - 1801. In a decayed state though now stabilised. Wave-form mantling subgroup. Church now with Redundant Churches' Fund.

47. HACKTHORN, St. Michael (L) :
On the west wall of the nave over the gallery. Moulded / cast in plaster and painted white as wall. Good condition. Modern Arms presumably contemporary with the building of the church in 1844 - 1851.

48. HALTHAM-ON-BAIN, St. Benedict (L) :
Painted high up on the boarding which
forms the east wall of the tower.
Rectangular c. 8' 6" by 5'. Fair
condition. Stuart Arms with 'C R' across
top which would seem to confirm a date
in the reign of Charles I. The set has
been treated very decoratively with its
edges bounded by columns hung with
drapery, and the royal helm depicted as
a pair of scallop shells. Both top and
bottom of the boards have been lost,
only half of the crest is now left and
the motto ribbon is hard against the
lower edge. There has also been
considerable paint loss on the surface,
leaving only red, black, white and the
underpainting of gold visible. Church
now with Redundant Churches' Fund.

49. HARLAXTON, SS Mary and Peter (K) :
On nave north wall. Painted on a canvas
quatrefoil (Plates 11 and 25). Arms of
1801 - 1816 with 'G de Ligne Gregory
Esq. Rev H Dodwell Rector. Rev Thos.
Haskett & T Harvey Chwardens' on lower
lobe. No mantling but the whole Arms
enclosed by a red and ermine cloak with
a second crest of the Prince of Wales'
feathers above and set against a
skyscape background. Good condition
though in need of restretching.

Plate 24. Detail of the Arms of
1801 - 1816 at Harlaxton church.

50. HARMSTON, All Saints (K) :
Above the tower screen. Painted on
canvas over wood in a heavy classical
frame c.3' each side and in need of
cleaning. Arms of 1714 - 1801 with 'G R'
above Arms and inscription beneath on
painted plinth 'This church was in a
falling down condition & ye chancel wch
was quite down were Rebuilt Anno Dom.
1717 at ye sole charge of the Right
Honble Sir George Thorold Bart. Ld
Mayor'.

51. HARPSWELL, St. Chad (L) :
On the north wall of the nave. Painted
on boards; 52" square with 5" frame.
Arms of 1702 - 1707 with date 1703 in
bottom left hand corner. Mid bottom a
roundel with flowing and interlocked
'A R' and around in garter-like manner
'PRO.DEI.GLORIA.ET.ECCLESIA.SALUTE'. The
base to the Arms hung with painted swags
of fruit and drapery. Fine set with
extensive use of gilding. Wave-form
mantling subgroup. Recently cleaned
(1977) by Miss Anna Hulbert.

52. HAUGHAM, All Saints (L) :
Above the chancel arch. Cast metal, cf.
Nettleton, painted and gilded. Arms of
post 1837 (probably 1840 when church was
built) in good condition - type II
complete. Church now with Redundant
Churches' Fund.

53. HEMSWELL, All Saints (L) :
On the west wall of the nave. Painted on
boards; 3' square with 4" frame (Plate
26). Arms of 1801 - 1837 but with no
crown in the middle of the escutcheon of
pretence. Very dull - needs cleaning.
This set is the work of two different
artists. The shield and helm are
considerably cruder than the supporters,
base, motto and mantling and the two
areas show up quite differently in a
raking light. The supporters and other
ancillaries are very much in the style
of Pudsey of Gainsborough who painted
the late C18th sets at Kettlethorpe and
Newton on Trent. It seems likely that
the shield was also originally by Pudsey
and that it was repainted subsequently
to update the heraldry. The resulting
shield is very crude with numerous
mistakes in the heraldry, the crown or
bonnet over the inescutcheon for example
resembles a beehive, and the lion of
Scotland is depicted as a blue horse.
In her report following cleaning tests
carried out in 1977 the restorer, Anna
Hulbert, noted that the helm over the
Arms had been painted to resemble a
diver's helmet! The Arms is signed in
pencil on the unicorn's flank 'I
Hawkworth Painter Gainsboro 1837', and
since the Arms have been repainted to
the heraldry, albeit approximately, of
that period this must be the signature
of the second artist. Pudsey's two Arms
are signed and it is possible that his

48

Plate 26. Arms of 1801 - 1837 at Hemswell church - taken in raking light.

signature may be found on this one on cleaning. John Hawksworth of Beast Market, Gainsborough is listed as a painter in White's 1826 Directory together with William P. Pudsey of Great Church Lane. In 1842 John Hawksworth Painter was at Spring Gardens Gainsborough (White 1842) and in 1849 John Hawksworth was listed as a painter and coal merchant in Beast Market with his home address in Trinity Street, Gainsborough (Hager 1849). The same name appears in White's 1856 Directory under the heading 'Painters (House, sign etc)' with an address in Market Street, Gainsborough.

54. HOLBEACH, All Saints (Ho) :
In nave above the north door. Painted on canvas c.5' side. Arms of 1714 - 1801 with 'G II R' above Arms. In good condition with mantling of ermine and or.

55. HORBLING, St. Andrew (K) :
Above the chancel arch. Painted on wood c.4' square. Arms of 1714 - 1801 in good condition. Background and mantling painted red. Foliage swags under the motto.

56. HORKSTOW, St. Maurice (Hu) :
Painting on canvas over boards - lozenge-shaped, 5' 2" square. Fairly well preserved. Arms of 1714 - 1801 with 'G R' in the top corner and 18..21 in the middle corners. The date must be an addition to the Arms. Wave-form mantling subgroup. Bonney's notes state that 'The King's Arms are at the West end of the nave.' Currently (1989) being restored in Lincoln.

57. HUMBERSTON, St. Peter (Hu) :
On the west face of the tower above the opening into the nave. Painted on canvas c.2' square. Stuart Arms of 1702 - 07. In good condition with the 'Semper Eadem' motto for Queen Anne. A fine set with extensive use of gilding. This set was noted by Loft in his notes of 1826 - 7 [LAO Dixon 19/1/2 f.17-20].

58. IMMINGHAM, St. Andrew (Hu) :
Over the chancel arch. Painting on canvas - about 6 feet square. Well preserved and recently cleaned. Stuart Arms with 'FEAR GOD HONOUR ye KING' across the top and above the Arms
'1688
J2   R'
Arms of James II are uncommon and it is unusual to find the initial 'J' used instead of 'I'. Noted by Ross c. 1830 [LAO Ross MSS vol. III f.204]. Wave-form mantling subgroup. See back cover for illustration of this Arms.

59. INGOLDMELLS, SS. Peter and Paul (L):
On the north wall of the tower base. Painted on canvas. Venetian window shape of c. 70" side including frame. Semi-circle above containing a dove. In fair condition although some blistering of the paint at the lower edge. Arms of 1816 - 1837 with Tudor roses with thistles and two medallions on the motto ribbon. Before the 1939 restoration it hung on the east wall of the nave over the demolished chancel arch where marks of its former location may still be seen, cf. Addlethorpe.

60. IRNHAM, St. Andrew (K) :
On nave north wall. Painted on wood on lozenge with c.4' side. Arms of 1714 - 1801 with 'G R' above and 'W P' and 'I S' to left and right and the date '1726' on the panel beneath the motto. There is an error in the Hanover quarter where the Arms of Scotland appear instead of those of Luneburgh. Very similar Arms at Corby Glen.

61. KETTLETHORPE, St. Peter and St. Paul (L) :
Over the tower arch / entrance. Painted on canvas with wood behind - 3' square, in frame. Good condition. Arms of 1801 - 1816 (Plate 27). Along bottom 'W. P. Pudsey. Painter Gainsborough 1812'. cf. Newton-on-Trent also signed by Pudsey and he was also probably responsible for the altered Arms at Hemswell (see above No. 53). Wm P. Pudsey is listed as a painter in 1826, in Great Church Lane, Gainsborough [White 1826] but his name does not appear in directories after that date.

Plate 27. Arms in Kettlethorpe church.

62. KIRKBY-CUM-OSGODBY, St. Andrew (L) :
On the north side of the tower arch. Painting on boards - rectangular 4' 6" wide and 3' 6" tall. Fairly well preserved (woodworm active). Arms of 1714 - 1801 with 'G 2d R' across the top. Wave-form mantling subgroup.

63. KIRKBY-ON-BAIN, St. Andrew (L) :
On the west wall of the nave. Painting on 5 vertical boards some 6' square but fairly dull. The boards have shrunk and have been filled in in a clumsy way. Arms of 1707 - 1714 - Queen Anne after the Union with Scotland. Across the Arms 'Fear God Honour the Queen 1712 A R' and the usual 'Semper Eadem'.

64. KIRKBY UNDERWOOD, St. Mary and All Saints (K) :
On tower north wall. Painted on canvas c.4' square. Arms of 1714 - 1801. In a neglected and dingy condition. 'Wm. Brittain Ch-Warden' beneath Arms.

65. LEASINGHAM, St. Andrew (K) :
On tower north wall. Painted on canvas c.3' side. Arms of 1801 - 1816 in good condition though the paint on the lion supporter has become marked by damp. Tudor roses and thistles as badges in base. Backing to the motto ribbon resembles that at Ingoldmells.

66. LEVERTON, St. Helen (Ho) :
On nave north wall. Painted on wood in octagon c.5' wide. Arms of 1714 - 1801 with 'W IV R' above Arms and '1823' beneath (Plate 22c) Sound condition but hung very high up on the west wall of the nave. Wave-form mantling subgroup. Details of the shield such as the turned back edge are close to the Arms at Barton-on-Humber.

67. LINCOLN, St. Benedict (L) :
On chancel north wall and painted on wood c.5' square. Arms of 1714 - 1801 cleaned in 1976. Along bottom : 'J. Harrison and J. Jellif Churchwardens 1734 Iohn Kirton Churchwarden in the year 1819' Wave-form mantling subgroup. The Churchardens' Accounts for October 1734 include payments of 18s 2d for the 'bord' for the Arms and £1 11s 6d 'For the Kings Armes'. Crossed out beneath are the same sums and the name, 'Samll White', as the supplier of the board, but with no reference to the painter of the Arms. [LAO Lincoln St. Benedict Par. Churchwardens Accounts 1715 - 56] Photos of the church published 1929 - 32 show the Arms at the west end of the nave between two arch-headed Commandment boards [LAO Ex 17/2].

68. LONG BENNINGTON, St. Swithun (K) :
Above the chancel arch. Painted on canvas with c.3' side. Arms of 1714 - 1801 in good condition. 'G II R' above the Arms and '1737' beneath (Plate 28). The base under the supporters' feet painted to resemble marble. Mantling ermine and or. A somewhat crude but vigorous set - see also Foston, Stragglethorpe and Westborough.

Plate 28. Arms in Long Bennington church.

69. MARKET RASEN, St. Thomas (L) :
Fixed onto iron gates in the tower arch. Cast metal about 18" wide. Recently repainted (Plate 14). Arms of post 1837, Type 1 complete.

70. MELTON ROSS, Holy Ascension (Hu) :
High on west wall of nave. Painted on wood about 3' square. Well preserved Arms of 1714 - 1801 with 'G R III' across the top and '17...74' across the middle (Plate 29). LAO Faculty Book 2, p.37 - 39 dated 1773 records a faculty for the building of a new church at Melton - a Georgian building which was destroyed in 1867 when the present church was constructed. Presumably the Arms were made for the Georgian church.

Plate 29. Arms in Melton Ross church.

71. MIDVILLE, St. Peter (L) :
On gallery. Cast metal Arms, type 1 - painted. Arms of 1816 - 1837. The church was built in 1819 so this is probably the date of the Arms, cf. Carrington and Frithville.

72. MOULTON, All Saints (Ho) :
Not hung. Painted on canvas c.3' 6" square. Post 1837 Arms signed 'H. J. Watts' and 'F. Oldenshaw'. Probably painted to commemorate the Silver Jubilee of Queen Elizabeth II in 1977.

73. NAVENBY, St. Peter (K) :
Above the tower arch. Painted on wood c.4' side. Arms of 1707 - 1714 in good condition. 'Feare God Honour Ye Queen' and 'A R' above Arms. 'ANTHONY FOUNTAIN CHURCH WARDEN, Thomas Hunton of Lincoln, Painter 1710' on plinth painted beneath supporters' feet. Found amongst lumber and restored to the church in 1910 (church guide). Wave-form mantling subgroup. Mantling ermine and or.

74. NETTLEHAM, All Saints (L) :
Above the chancel arch. Painted on canvas about 3' square in new condition (Plate 8). Arms of 1816 - 1837 with signature of local artist Chris Broddle in bottom right corner. He repainted the Arms using photographs of the original after the latter was lost in the fire of 1969. The escutcheon of the crown of Charlemagne is missing and the motto is painted across the ribbon without regard to its folds. The church guide includes photographs of both of the Arms and its position over the chancel arch with accompanying panels of Commandents. The lion's face is very human.

75. NETTLETON, St. John the Baptist (L):
High on the west wall of the nave. Well preserved Arms of post 1837 in cast metal and painted. Type II complete.

76. NEWTON ON TRENT, St. Peter (L) :
High above chancel arch. Painted on canvas in lozenge-manner, about 4' along each side. Arms of 1714 - 1801. Needs cleaning and hard to see. Signed 'Pudsey....Gainsbro' 1792'. Related to Arms at Kettlethorpe and Hemswell.

77. NORTH THORESBY, St. Helen (L) :
Not hung but stored on gallery in the base of the tower. Painted on boards - lozenge-shaped, 4' 3" square. Fairly well preserved. Arms of 1714 - 1801 with '1722' in the top corner and 'G..R' in the middle corners. Mantling represented as heavy folds of fabric.

78. NORTON DISNEY, St. Peter (K) :
On nave south wall. Painted on canvas c.5' square. Arms of 1714 - 1801 marked by damp and in need of cleaning. 'G III R' above Arms.

79. ORBY IN THE MARSH, All Saints, (L):
Over the north door of the nave. Painted on boards - rectangular, 5' 3" wide by 4' 2" high. Arms of 1714 -1801 in fair condition with 'G. R. 3' above Arms and in the bottom right corner 'J. Burnitt Painter 1781'. Wave-form mantling subgroup with mantling ermine and or.

80. OSBOURNBY, St. Peter and St. Paul (K) :
Nave west end under the tower arch. Painted on canvas c.4' by 3'. Arms of 1714 - 1801. 'G R' above Arms and '1797' in base. Wave-form mantling subgroup. Signed lower right, 'Phillips'. Mantling ermine and or with heavy curtains pulled back at the top of the board to reveal the Arms. Further panels of Moses and Aaron and the Commandments signed 'T. Phillips Pinx Bourn' also in the nave.

81. OWSTON FERRY, St. Martin, (Hu) :
Over the north door of the nave. Painted on five boards running vertically - rectangular, 4' 7" tall, 3' 7" wide in gilded 9" wide frame. Very dull. Arms of Queen Anne 1707 - 1714, i.e. after the Union with Scotland. The motto below reads, 'Semper Aeadem'.

82. RAITHBY BY LOUTH, St. Peter, (L) :
On the west gallery. Cast metal, type 1 complete. Good condition, well painted but with blue mantling. Arms of post 1837.

83. RIPPINGALE, St. Andrew (K) :
On tower north wall. Painted on canvas c.4' square. Unidentified Arms completely obscured.

84. ROWSTON, St. Clement (K) :
In vestry. Painted on wood c.3' side. Arms of 1714 - 1801 with 'G R II' above Arms. This set formed part of a reredos in the chancel, occupying the centre position under a triangular cornice. When examined in 1978 the reredos had been dismantled and was in a neglected and deteriorating state. Since then it has been restored by Anna Hulbert. The reredos is dated 1741 and there are names painted on the lower edge, inaccessible in 1978.

85. SAXBY ALL SAINTS, All Saints (Hu) :
On nave north wall. Cast metal Arms of post 1837 (Plate 18). Type II painted. Bonney ; 1846 noted the Arms set up in front of the gallery.

86. SCAWBY, St. Hybald (Hu) :
On west gallery in the nave. Cast metal Arms of post 1837 (Plate 19). Type III complete and painted.

87. SCOTHERN, St. German (L) :
On the east wall of the north chapel. Painted on canvas - 41" square. Fair, dull condition. Arms of 1714 - 1801 with '17 96' in bottom corners. The Arms are towards the bottom of the painting with above, open drapes revealing landscape and sky. No mantling. Cleaned in 1940s and it would justify further cleaning.

88. SNELLAND, All Saints (L) :
Hanging on the north wall of the north aisle. Cast metal and mounted on a cartouche shaped board on which is painted 'V R'. Arms of post 1837, well painted. Type 1 complete.

89. SOMERSBY, St. Margaret (L) :
Above south door. Probably cast metal, finely moulded Arms of 1714 - 1801 and in very good condition (See front cover and Plate 9). Painted in many colours - about 2' square. Mantling ermine and or.

90. SOUTH CARLTON, St. John the Baptist (L) :
Over the tower arch with a hatchment at each side. Painted on canvas - lozenge shaped c. 4' each side. Good condition but no mantling. Arms of 1801 - 1816. Churchwardens' Accounts for 1815 - 16 include payments of 3 gns to Patrick Shee of Newark on Trent for painting the Royal Arms with a further payment of 14s to Joseph Coxon for making the frame for the Arms and hanging it.[LAO S. Carlton Par. Churchwardens' Accounts 1775 / 1823]. Notes added to the Register of Baptisms and Births for 1766 - 1812 [LAO S/Car, 13] refer to the payment to Patrick O'Shee (sic) and add that the Arms were installed in 1816 to replace a Queen Anne set that had been put up in 1707 and removed in 1812.

91. SOUTH KELSEY, St. Mary (L) :
High up over the tower arch. Appears to be painted on canvas - about 2' 6" square. Fairly well preserved. Arms of 1816 - 1837 with 'G R IV' across the top.

92. STAMFORD, St. Martin (K) :
Canvas lozenge c. 4' side in good condition. Arms of 1801 - 1816 with 'G R' left and right of centre and date '1808' painted over '1758' in base (Plate 30). Mantling ermine and or. The style of the supporters and base motto would support a mid 18th century date and would suggest that the shield had been repainted to update the heraldry.

Plate 30. Detail of Georgian Arms at St. Martin's church, Stamford.

93. STIXWOULD, St. Peter (L) :
Above the chancel arch. Cast metal Arms
of 1801 - 1837. Painted unheraldically.
Type I complete. Royal Arms dated 1662
was removed from parish church and
displayed in Abbey farm [J. C. Hine
Records of Parishes around Horncastle,
1904].

94. STRAGGLETHORPE, St. Michael (K) :
Nave, south wall . Painted on canvas c.
3' square. Arms of 1714 - 1801 with 'G
R' at top. Dingy and in need of
cleaning. Error in Hanover where
Brunswick has gained an extra lion. See
also Foston, Long Bennington and
Westborough.

95. SURFLEET, St. Laurence (Ho) :
On nave north wall. Painted on canvas
c.4' square. Arms of 1707 - 1714 in good
condition (Plate 7). 'A R' above Arms
and 'G R IV' in base with motto 'Semper
Eadem'. Mantling depicted as elegant
sways of stylised foliage in ermine and
or.

96. SUTTERTON, St. Mary the Virgin (Ho):
Over the north aisle door. Painted on
canvas c. 4' square. Arms of Elizabeth
II signed 'Terry Despight 1981'.

97. SUTTON BRIDGE, St. Matthew (Ho) :
On nave west wall. Carved, perhaps of
Coade stone. Arms of post 1837 and c.4'
across. Painted with red and gold
mantle behind Arms and silver edged
mantling above.

98. TEALBY, All Saints (L) :
Inside the tower on the north wall. Arms
are shaped like the gable end of a house
- 7' from apex to base, sides of 4' and
width 8'. Painted on boards 10 - 12"
wide which run from top to bottom. Arms
of 1816 - 1837 with what appears to be a
crown over the central Arms of Hanover
[but these Arms have no central ?bonnet
in shield above the horse.] 'G III R' at
the top of the Arms. Badly faded and
some of paint has dropped off. Loft
(1826-27) noted the King's Arms over the
west gallery of the nave with the
Commandments on two panels above the
chancel arch [LAO Dixon 19/1/2 f.1 - 21]

99. THORNTON CURTIS, St. Lawrence (H) :
On the west wall of the nave above the
tower arch. Painted on canvas c.4' by
c.3' and in sound condition. Arms of
1714 - 1801 with 'G 3 R' above Arms and
'G. 3rd 1768 V. R. 1887' on the lower
edge of the frame - the latter date
presumably marking the end of the
church's restoration in that year. A
rather crude set (Plate 21a) with errors
in the heraldry. The lion of Scotland
has lost its tressure and has become a
griffin; in the Hanover quarter the
Luneburgh semee of hearts is missing;
Brunswick has gained an extra lion and
the Westphalia section and the crown of
Charlemagne have been omitted.

100. THORPE ST PETER, St Peter (L) :
Over tower arch. Painting on boards.
Rectangular c. 6' by 5'. In poor
condition with large cracks in the
panels - needs cleaning. Arms of 1714 -
1801 with 'G R' above. Wave-form
mantling subgroup.

101. THURLBY BY BOURNE, St. Germain (K) :
In south porch. Carved and painted Arms
of 1816 - 1837 in good condition.

102. TOYNTON ALL SAINTS, All Saints (L):
On west wall of nave. Painted on canvas
- 5' square with 'loaf' shaped extension
on top. Arms of 1801 - 1816. Nicely
framed and in fairly good condition.
Across the bottom of the Arms - 'WILLIAM
BARKER 1831 CHURCH WARDEN'. Inscription
looks contemporary with the Arms rather
than added but certainly they appear to
be of 1801 - 1816. Mantling ermine and
or.

103. TRUSTHORPE, St. Peter (L) :
Above west gallery. Painted on boards -
lozenge-shaped Arms c.4' side. Arms of
post 1837 in fair condition with 'V R'
above Arms and '1842' beneath.
Supporters shown crawling from behind
shield and mantling omitted.

104. WAINFLEET ST MARY, St Mary (L) :
Over the tower arch. Painting on canvas.
Massive rectangular Arms c. 6' wide and
c.8' high. Very dirty. Arms of 1816 -
1837. No helm or mantling above the
achievement, only large crown and
crowned lion. Lion supporter rampant,
unicorn supporter crawling from behind
the shield. Error in Hanover quarter
with the Arms of Scotland instead of
those of Luneburgh.

105. WASHINGBOROUGH, St. John Evangelist
(K) :
On nave west wall. Painted on canvas,
Arms of 1714 - 1801. Shaped to fit an
arch c.10' wide and c.4' high at apex,
but with lower edge lost. Good condition
with 'G R' in elaborate script beneath
the shield. Feet of both supporters and
the motto ribbon missing (Plate 21d).

106. WELL, St. Margaret (L) :
On front of east gallery (altar is at
west end of church). Painting on canvas
in gilt frame. Rectangular 2' 3" wide
by 2' high. Good condition. Arms of
1714 - 1801 with 'G II R' above the
Arms. Error in Hanover quarter where
crown of Charlemagne has changed colour
with its ground. Wave-form mantling
subgroup. Mantling ermine and or.

107. WELTON-BY-LINCOLN, St. Mary (L) :
On west wall of the nave. Lozenge shape
c. 4' 6" sides (Plate 31). Appears to
be painted on canvas - good condition.
Arms of 1801 - 1816 with '1838' in
bottom corner. Mantling ermine and or.

Plate 31. Arms in Welton church.

108. WESTBOROUGH, All Saints (K) :
Above the tower arch. Painted on wood
c.3' by 4' in Venetian window form. Arms
of 1714 - 1801 with 'G II R' above Arms
and date '1757' at lower left and right
(Plate 5). Mantling ermine and or.
Error in Hanover quarter with an extra
lion in the Brunswick section. Fine and
spirited set. See also Foston, Long
Bennington and Stragglethorpe.

109. WHAPLODE, St. Mary (Ho) :
Above the chancel arch. Painted on
canvas c.3' by c4'. Arms of 1714 - 1801
in good condition. 'G R III 1773' above
Arms. 'R Weston (?) R Pearse (?) Church
wardens BULLARD Painter' on the lower
edge. Mantling ermine and or.

110. WOOTTON, St. Andrew (Hu) :
Above the chancel arch. Sheet metal
Arms c.2' diameter. Arms of post 1837.
This set consists of only the shield
with the crown above, surrounded by
garter motto and 'Feare God Honor Ye
Kyng'. Most probably early twentieth
century.

111. WYBERTON, St. Leodegar (Ho) :
On tower north wall. Wood lozenge c.3'
6" each side in a neglected and dingy
state. Arms of 1714 - 1801 with 'G R'
in upper angle. Possibly wave-form
mantling subgroup.

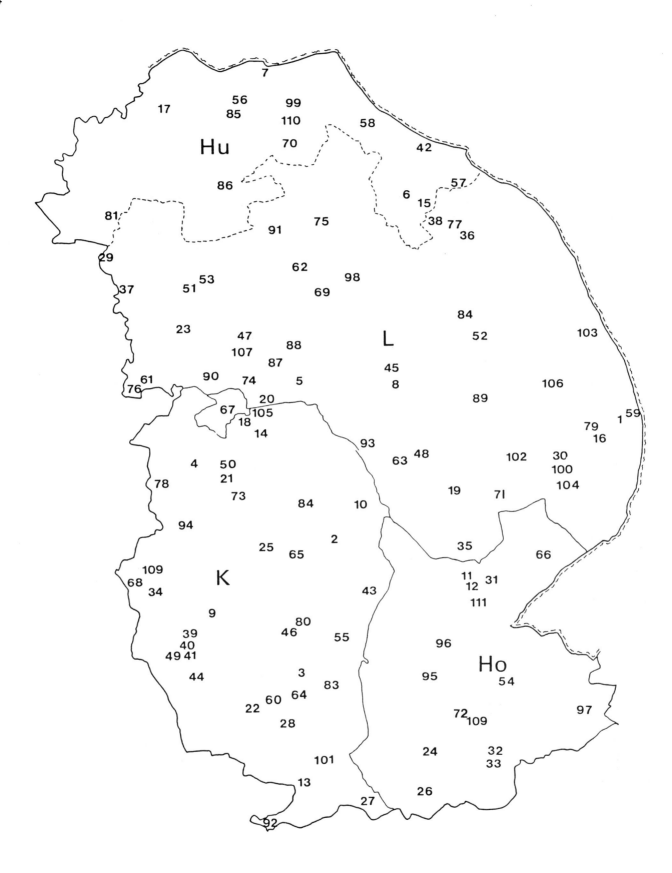

Fig. 2. Map locating all surviving Royal Arms
in Lincolnshire churches

1. Addlethorpe (1714 - 1801)
2. Anwick (1708)
3. Aslackby (1714 - 1801)
4. Aubourn (1733)
5. Barlings (1739)
6. Barnoldby le Beck (1801 - 1816)
7. Barton-on-Humber (G R II)
8. Baumber (1714 - 1801)
9. Belton by Grantham (1816 - 1837)
10. Billinghay (1801)
11. Boston 1 (C R)
12. Boston 2 (1816 - 1837)
13. Braceborough (1714 - 1801)
14. Branston (1816 - 1837)
15. Brigsley (1819)
16. Burgh le Marsh (1714 - 1801)
17. Burton-on-Stather (G R III)
18. Canwick (post 1837)
19. Carrington (1816 - 1837)
20. Cherry Willingham (1801 - 1816)
21. Coleby (1801 - 1816)
22. Corby Glen (1714 - 1801)
23. Cotes-by-Stow (1635)
24. Cowbit (1713)
25. Cranwell (G R II)
26. Crowland (1775)
27. Deeping St. James (1801 - 1816)
28. Edenham (1820)
29. East Stockwith (post 1837)
30. Firsby (1736)
31. Fishtoft (post 1837)
32. Fleet 1 (1698)
33. Fleet 2 (1867)
34. Foston (1767)
35. Frithville (1816 - 1837)
36. Fulstow (1768)
37. Gainsborough (post 1837)
38. Grainsby (1714 - 1801)
39. Grantham 1 St. Wulfram's (1586)
40. Grantham 2   "   (C R II)
41. Grantham 3. St. John (1848)
42. Great Grimsby (1714 - 1801)
43. Great Hale (1801)
44. Great Ponton (G R III)
45. Great Sturton (1808)
46. Haceby (1714 - 1801)
47. Hackthorn (post 1837)
48. Haltham-on-Bain (C R)
49. Harlaxton (1801 - 1816)
50. Harmston (1717)
51. Harpswell (1703)
52. Haugham (post 1837)
53. Hemswell (1801 - 1837)
54. Holbeach (G R II)
55. Horbling (1714 - 1801)
56. Horkstow (1714 - 1801)
57. Humberston (1702 - 1707)
58. Immingham (1688)
59. Ingoldmells (1816 - 1837)
60. Irnham (1726)
61. Kettlethorpe (1812)
62. Kirkby-cum-Osgodby (G R II)
63. Kirkby-on-Bain (1712)
64. Kirkby Underwood (1714 - 1801)
65. Leasingham (1801 - 1816)
66. Leverton (1714 - 1801)
67. Lincoln, St. Benedict (1734)
68. Long Bennington (1737)
69. Market Rasen (post 1837)
70. Melton Ross (1774)
71. Midville (1816 - 1837)
72. Moulton (post 1837)
73. Navenby (1710)
74. Nettleham (1816 - 1837)
75. Nettleton (post 1837)
76. Newton on Trent (1792)
77. North Thoresby (1722)
78. Norton Disney (G R III)
79. Orby in the Marsh (1781)
80. Osbournby (1797)
81. Owston Ferry (1707 - 1714)
82. Raithby by Louth (post 1837)
83. Rippingale (no date)
84. Rowston (G R II)
85. Saxby All Saints (post 1837)
86. Scawby (post 1837)
87. Scothern (1796)
88. Snelland (V R)
89. Somersby (1714 - 1801)
90. South Carlton (1816)
91. South Kelsey (G R IV)
92. Stamford (1808 over 1758)
93. Stixwould (1801 - 1837)
94. Stragglethorpe (1714 - 1801)
95. Surfleet (A R)
96. Sutterton (1981)
97. Sutton Bridge (post 1837)
98. Tealby (G R III)
99. Thornton Curtis (G R III)
100. Thorpe St. Peter (1714 - 1801)
101. Thurlby by Bourne (1816 - 1837)
102. Toynton All Saints (1801 - 1816)
103. Trusthorpe (1842)
104. Wainfleet St. Mary (1816 - 1837)
105. Washingborough (1714 - 1801)
106. Well (G R II)
107. Welton-by-Lincoln (1801 - 1816)
108. Westborough (1757)
109. Whaplode (1773)
110. Wootton (post 1837)
111. Wyberton (1714 - 1801)

Table of surviving Royal Arms in Lincolnshire churches -
the numbers relate to the Figure 2 map and the Inventory
in Chapter 8.

9.

Bibliography

General :

Cautley, H. M., 1934. Royal Arms and Commandments in our Churches (Ipswich)
Hasler, C., 1980. The Royal Arms (London)
Petchey, W.J., 1962. Armorial Bearings of the Sovereigns of England (London)
* Pardoe, R., 1987. Royal Arms in Churches : The Artists and Craftsmen.

There are many publications dealing with Arms in particular counties or towns - here are a selection :

Bretton, R., 1941.'Royal Arms in Our Churches' (The Old Parish of Halifax), in Transactions of the Halifax Antiquarian Society 1941 p. 37 - 55
Bretton, R., 1955 'Royal Arms in Our Churches' (The Old Parish of Halifax), in Transactions of the Halifax Antiquarian Society 1955, pp 91 - 94.
Briscoe, J.P., 1892-93. 'Royal Arms in Churches', in Notts and Derbyshire Notes and Queries 1, pp 53 - 4.
Hunter Blair, C. H. and Evetts, L. C., 1953. 'Royal Arms in Parish Churches of Northumberland and Durham', in Archaeologia Aeliana 31 pp. 48 - 68.
Evetts, L. C., 1964. 'Royal Arms in Churches', in Care of Churches, pp. 32 - 37.
Fawcett, E., 1937 -9. 'The Royal Arms and Achievements in Somerset Churches', in Somerset Arch. and Nat. Hist. Soc. 1937 - 1939.
Jeavons, S.A., 1963. 'Royal Arms in Derbyshire Churches', in Derbyshire Archaeological Journal Vol. LXXXIII, pp. 51 - 65.
Jeavons, S.A., 1962. 'Royal Arms in Staffordshire Churches', in Transactions of Birmingham Archaeological Society 78, pp.86 - 95.
MacCulloch, D., 1971. 'Royal Arms in Suffolk Churches', in Proceedings of the Suffolk Institute of Archaeology 32, part 2, pp. 193-7. This article lists additions and amendments to the list of Arms in Suffolk churches in Cautley, H. M. 1934.
Morgan, P., 1955. 'Royal Arms in Warwickshire Churches', in Transactions of Birmingham Archaeological Society 71, pp. 41 - 58.
Morgan, P., 1956. 'Royal Arms in Worcestershire Churches', in Transcations of Worcestershire Archaeological Society New Series XXXII, pp. 20 - 35.

* A large number of booklets have been published privately by Rosemary Pardoe and can be obtained from her (when still in print) at Flat One, 36 Hamilton Street, Hoole, Chester CH2 3JQ. These include County Surveys of Arms in Bedfordshire & Hertfordshire, Cambridgeshire and Huntingdonshire, Cornwall, Devon, Essex, Central London, Northamptonshire, Nottinghamshire, Oxfordshire, Shropshire, and Yorkshire.

Other references

White, W. and Parson, W. (Ed), 1826. Lincolnshire Directory.
White, W., 1842. Lincolnshire Directory.
White, W., 1856. Lincolnshire Directory.
Hager and Co., 1849. Commercial Directory of the Market Towns in Lincolnshire.